Personal CNC Routing

HOW TO USE A CNC ROUTER

A PRACTICAL GUIDE FOR BEGINNERS

by

DENNIS KEELING

For Enthusiasts, Hobbyists and Model Makers

New 2022 revised edition

This is the update of the early editions of the CNC Router series. This is not a workshop manual.

This is an introductory booklet for hobbyists and model makers thinking of using a CNC Router for the first time.

Contents

Acknowledgement

Supplier of CNC equipment:- www.ltcnc.cn

Supplier of CAD software: http://www.solidworks.com

Supplier of CAM software: http://www.vectric.com

Supplier of CNC Control System: http://www.machsupport.com

DEDICATION

To my wife Lyndsey, my sons, grandsons and friends.

INTRODUCTION

Operating a CNC Router is simple - the skill is in creating a design that works and specifying the way it has to be machined.

When I first started to use a CNC Router in 2012 at university, I found it very difficult to understand the process and even more difficult to understand how to operate a CNC. As a furniture design student I was taught how to design in CAD, but there was no training given on how to use the manufacturing software (CAM) to feed the information to the CNC, or how to use the CNC's control system to operate the CNC. This was outside the scope of the course.

Fig 1: The technician cutting my sculptured seat at University

There were technical books on the subject but nothing for the non-engineering student or home enthusiast. After I finished my course I wanted to have my own CNC router to continue using the CNC.

Was I unique being a home enthusiast?—Definitely not, as I soon found the various forums that exist in this community. But what I found was that there were very few 'how-to' books for the hobbyist or model maker.

Designing in CAD (Computer Aided Design) seemed quite straightforward but I realized I knew very little about how to operate CAM (Computer Aided Manufacturing) and how to control the CNC with the CNC Control System. I therefore decided, that when I felt competent enough, I would write a book to explain these stages to hobbyists like myself.

So this is not a technical guide that explains the intricacies of G-Code and advanced engineering - it is just me, a home enthusiast, explaining what I have learnt over the past few years about operating a CNC Router, for other home enthusiasts.

Overview

Computer Numerically Controlled (CNC) machines have been around for many years, but only recently have these devices become affordable by the hobbyist. The most popular hobbyist machines today are the CNC Router, CNC Mill, CNC Laser Cutter and the 3D printer – all use similar techniques. In this book I will be focusing on how to use the CNC Router. See Fig Simple CNC Router below Fig 2.

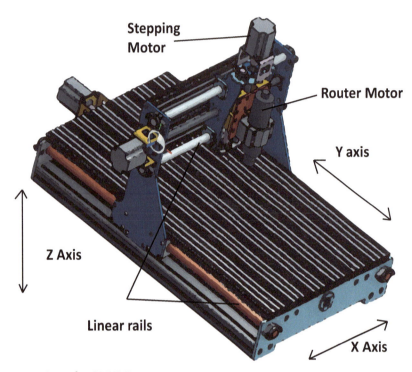

Fig 2: Simple CNC Router

A basic CNC Router has three axes – designated as X - Y - Z. This type of machine, called a flat bed, is used for two dimensional (2D) and three dimensional (3D) type of work. A fourth rotary axis machine can be configured for turned work like stair posts and spindles. The advanced 5 axis machine can be used for machining complex 3D structures, but that is outside the scope of this book. We will only consider the flat-bed machine in this book with its three X-Y-Z axes.

The CNC Router is not a stand-alone tool. It requires a stream of computer information to control it. The process for using a CNC Router starts from the design stage - which has to be in a digital form. A conventional pencil drawing has to be converted into a digital drawing first of all. CAD software is used for designing in a digital form. There are many sophisticated packages available costing a lot of money, like AutoCAD and Solidworks, but for the hobbyist there are a host of simple free tools available like SketchUp. However the output from the CAD package is rarely in the correct format to program the CNC.

The output from the CAD system, usually in the DXF format (AutoCAD Drawing Exchange Format) has to be modified in a CAM package to output in G-Code (numerical control (NC) programming language) to the CNC. It is this software package that the type of router cutter to be used is selected and the way the piece is to be machined. Again there are many cheap CAM packages available – some that will undertake both the CAD and the CAM elements in a single software package. I use the Vectric Cut2D package which has a comprehensive CAD section.

The output from the CAM package, referred to as G-Code, needs to be read by the computer control system associated with the CNC to tell it how to respond. A lot of CNC manufacturers have their own specially designed control system for their machine which take specialist forms of G-Code. A popular universal CNC control system is Mach3 from Artsoft which I prefer. It is used extensively by both hobbyists and professionals alike. There is a later version Mach4 which is really for more industrial use.

Selecting a CNC Router

CNC Routers can cost anything from a couple of hundred to over a hundred thousand dollars. As you would expect, price is not always the best means of selection. Some enthusiasts even make their own CNC, others buy off-the-shelf models, or like me, I had mine made cheaply to my specification in China. So what are the key criteria for selection? To understand the difference in prices one has to understand the method of construction and the components used.

Availablity

When buying a CNC you obviously get what you pay for. You cannot expect to get a rigid professional machine designed for furniture making for a couple of hundred dollars. But with imports from the far east, prices for the home enthusiast have been dropping considerably. It will all depend on what you want to make with your CNC. Most of the low-cost CNC machines are only suitable for engraving. I used one for an article I wrote about small desktop machines but it was not even man-enough to cut acrylic plastic with a 3mm diameter router. However makers of simple wooden models may not need the strength, rigidity, accuracy and associated industrial machines designed to cut more complex items.

On auction sites like eBay, there are hundreds of low-cost models to choose from. New locally made equipment; overseas imported equipment and used industrial equipment. Used industrial equipment can be very large and heavy often using old technology.

The technology has changed rapidly over the last few years with modern general purpose control systems resulting in cheaper smaller and more accurate machines. 10 years ago it was virtually unheard of to buy a personal CNC router - similar to PC's thirty years ago until Bill Gates designed the personal computer which most of us have today.

I could not afford to buy a locally made CNC when I bought my first CNC. I decided to buy a low-cost CNC direct from China. There is an excellent resource for buying from the far east - AliExpress [https://www.aliexpress.com/]. Fig 3 opposite.

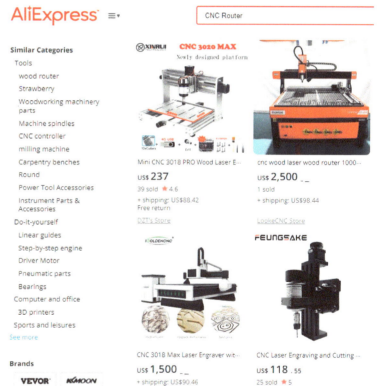

Fig3: AliExpress CNC Router search

I was able to configure my own specification and have it manufactured. My first CNC was made to order in 5 weeks, but it then took 2 months to be shipped from China and a further 2 months to get it working without any local support. I have now bought 4 CNCs all of them have had teething troubles as have the machines that two of my friends also bought. I did buy a CNC mill locally although it was manufactured in China, again it had teething troubles but they were quickly sorted out by a local representative. It was more expensive to buy locally but it saved all the hassle and the delivery was only a couple of days. A CNC is so complex that you usually need help to set up. My experience of Chinese machines is they are usually well made but the instructions have been badly translated. The Chinese are getting better with their instructions as more and more units are being shipped to the USA and Europe. I recently bought a CNC Laser Cutter and the instructions were excellent with a fully functional support website.

Construction

For those of you that have used a hand-held router you will know the forces and momentum behind the router motor when cutting at 15,000 rpm. It acts as a gyro - not wanting to change direction. Therefore to cut accurately, the router motor and the material to be machined need to be held firmly. Very often cheaper CNC Router machines are very flimsy and the router is allowed an undue amount of movement when it changes direction - called backlash.

Hand-held routers only cut in one direction - the router rotation against the direction of travel. But this is not the best direction for accurate cutting using a CNC - especially wood. A modern CNC Router will allow the cut to be in the 'climb' direction (rotation with the direction of travel) as well as the conventional rotation against the direction of travel. This needs the CNC to be of robust construction to fight against the cutting forces being exaggerated by the direction of travel.

There is an active market for kits to allow enthusiasts to build their own CNC router. Some CNCs are constructed out of MDF, (Fig4), this may be fine for model making. But when larger items are to be machined using larger router motors then rigidity becomes very important. Others are constructed from Aluminium channel which is in itself strong but the weakness lies in the way the channels are joined together.

Fig 4: DIY CNC Router in MDF

Fig 5: Unloading my first CNC Router

My first CNC had a 48" x 48" (1200mm x 1200mm) bed with a separate fourth axis for rotary work. It was so big I had to arrange for a crane to get it off the delivery lorry into my workshop. Just look at the size of the rotary chuck supplied with the 4th axis bed in the picture. Fig 5.

In those days I was planning to make furniture and cut spindles on my CNC. I gradually changed my mind on the things that I wanted to make. I became more interested in clock making so accuracy and rigidity were more important. My first CNC used a rack and pinion method of movement with the table static and a huge moving gantry which spanned the adjoining rotary table. It was great for making chair frames but not accurate 5: enough for clock making.

Having learned from my mistakes I then went in search of a smaller more accurate machine. There was no need for such a large bed so my replacement CNC had a smaller 24" x 24" (600mm x 600mm) cast iron bed and a fixed solid steel gantry. The table moved in the Y axis and the router on the gantry moving along the x axis and z axis. I even considered going to a servo motor version but my supplier suggested that it was not necessary for the accuracy as long as I invested in top quality linear bearings and ball screw linked stepping motors. The most important aspect of accuracy, I was informed, was to have a very rigid construction with a heavy cast-iron table. This CNC weighs in over 200Kg and is really robust - see opposite Fig 6.

Fig 6: Smaller replacement CNC

Axis Configuration

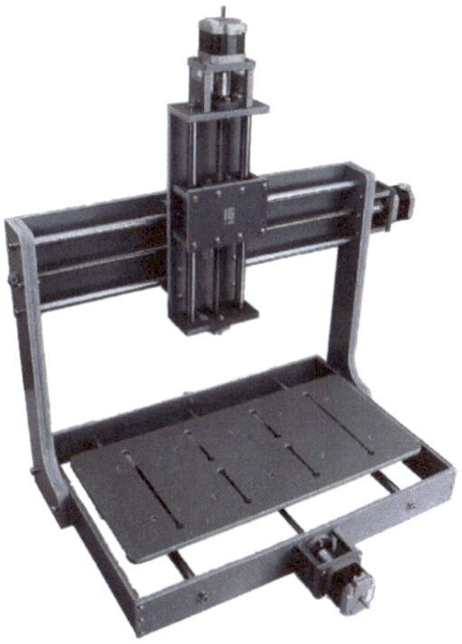

The basic function of the 3D CNC is to cut in three directions. This can be achieved by leaving the work-piece static with the router moving (static bed), or the opposite or any combination in between. The larger CNCs usually have a static bed with the router mounted on a gantry moving across the work in all directions. Small desktop machines usually have the bed moving in one direction Y (forwards and backwards) and the router, mounted in a fixed gantry, moving in the X (right and left) and Z (up and down) directions. To enable this movement the table and router need to move on rails. (Fig 7). The support bearings on these rails can be simple plastic bearings, or hardened steel rails with ball bearings or more expensive linear rails, (Fig 8), with composite ball bearings.

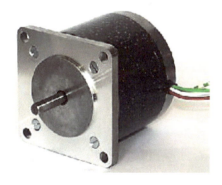

Fig 7: Simple Gantry setup

The table or the gantry and the router are moved by stepping motors or servo motors. There is usually one stepping motor in each direction although on some CNCs they may be operating in pairs. Stepping motors come in all sizes and configurations. It is essential that the stepping motor supplied can cope with the size of the work to be machined as well as the forces exerted by the gyroscopic effect of the router. The stepping motors are controlled by the micro-controller card. The more advance stepping motors use micro-stepping which enables greater accuracy and minimises backlash - see later.

Fig 8: Linear Rail

Fig 9: Stepping Motor

The rotary stepping-motor drives the axes by either a pinion gear or a threaded shaft. This connection can be made using a rubber band, a stepped cam belt, a direct mechanical gear, a chain (see below Fig 11) or a ball screw (Fig 10). On lighter CNCs like a 3D printer only a rubber band is used. But where a router is moved then the connection must be more substantial.

The small hobby 10"x8" CNC Router I used for an article had a rubber cam belt. My first 48"x48" CNC Router used a rack and pinion with a pair of stepping motors working together to drive the huge gantry. My new accurate 24" x 24" CNC Router has threaded rods and ball screws. See picture left. Fig 10.

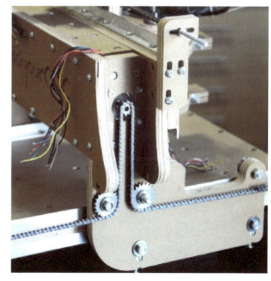

Fig 10: Ball Screw

Fig 11: Chain driven DIY gantry

Backlash

For those of you old enough to remember driving old bangers – they had 'play' in their steering – called backlash. You could turn the steering wheel several degrees without affecting the direction of travel - scary!

Modern rack and pinion construction is prone to these backlash problems - see the diagram opposite showing the play between the gear teeth of a typical rack & pinion rail. (Fig 12). Ball screws, on the other hand, have very little 'play' in them and can be very accurate.

Fig 12: Rack and pinion

Backlash manifests itself when the router has to change direction. For example cutting a circle where the router is changing direction continuously. My first big CNC could never cut a circle - it always turned out as an ellipse.

Eliminating backlash is one of the fundamental problems to overcome to achieve accurate CNC machining. Some CNC control systems can try to compensate for backlash but not usually very satisfactory. Some micro-stepping motors can minimise backlash.

A good test when buying a CNC is to have a 50mm disc cut with a 4mm centre hole. It will show up all the problems of the CNC. It will show the steps in the

Fig 13: Oval shape of backlash

side of the circle where it changes direction and possibly the elliptical effect of cutting a circle profile. (Fig 13). There isn't a lot that can be done with an existing CNC with a backlash problem, as I found out to my cost.

Material holding

The material has to be held securely for machining. It will depend on the bed of the CNC that you are using. Some DIY CNCs have a MDF bed with pre-set holes to locate hold-downs. Desktop machines usually have an aluminium bed with slots for the hold-downs - see picture Fig 14.

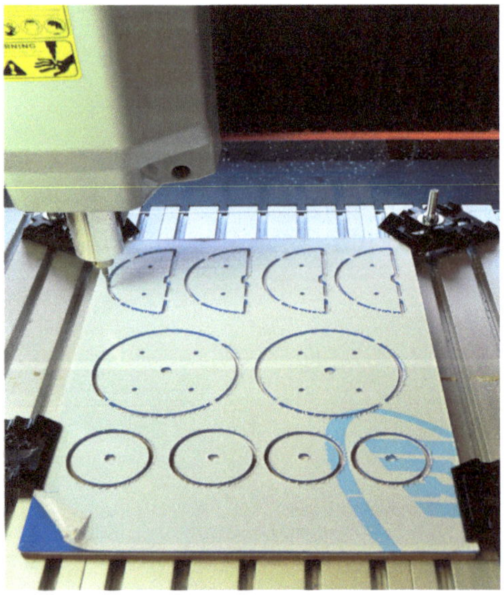

The forces exerted by the router during machining are considerable so the means of securing the material has to be rigid and fit for the type of machining being undertaken. The larger industrial router machines tend to use vacuum either as a vacuum table or as vacuum points. The smaller desktop router machines would use either a baseboard and glue, (Fig 15), or a metal base with slots for hold-downs to clamp the material. (Fig 14). Heavy pieces of material, especially metal blocks, would normally be clamped using mechanical means. Small wooden objects can be adequately secured by using hot-melt glue on a base-board. Sheet material and laminates like plastics are best held down with a vacuum table.

Fig 14: Mechanical hold-down

To enable the material to be machined to its full depth, a sacrificial baseboard is often used to allow the router to cut through the material without damaging the router table. I use 1/2" (12mm) MDF sheet as a sacrificial base. It has an even thickness and works with both mechanical and vacuum methods of material holding.

Fig 15: Baseboard and glue

Router Spindle Motor

Unfortunately router motors come in various sizes and capabilities. The majority of the CNC routers emanating from China are water cooled – not really necessary in northern climates. All too often the router motor supplied with small desktop machines is underpowered - really only suitable for engraving. If you want to cut a slot with a 10mm router cutter, then the router motor should have enough power to drive it. It's always worth upgrading to a router motor with more power rather than skimp on lower powered models. The small desktop machine that I used for an article had a 150 watt router – it couldn't machine acrylic with a 3mm cutter. I have a 2.2Kw router on my current small CNC which seems ideal for the work that I undertake. (Fig 16).

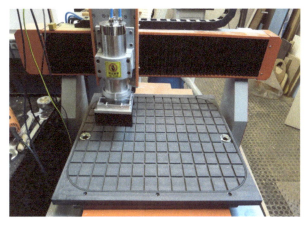

Fig16: CNC Router with Vacuum Table

Fig 17:Variable Speed Router & Inverter

Basic routers are usually fixed speed. For maximum control of your CNC a variable speed router is preferred - ideally controlled by the G-Code as the tool characteristics change. Some cutters require a slow speed some materials a high speed. I machine both plastics and wood and therefore I use a speed range from 10,000 - 25,000rpm.

Depending on the CNC some models will have a single phase router with basic speed control and diminishing power at lower speeds; but the more expensive CNCs will have a 3 phase router powered by an inverter to give more accurate speed control and more importantly, constant torque. Fig 17.

This brings with it certain requirements. A three phase router will maintain its speed better through different working conditions than a single phase router whose speed is proportional to the load imposed. The CNC control system should be able to send a signal to the router to not only switch it on and off but also to specify the rotational speed required. My first CNC could only set three different router speeds. My new CNC enables a variable speed range from 100 to 24,000 RPM to be selected by the control system. Others have an external speed control potentiometer mounted on the front panel.

The router motor usually has a collet chuck to mount the router cutters. I have an ER 20 collet clutch on my present CNC which allows me to select collet sizes from 1-13mm shank diameter. The ER 16 has a range of 1-10mm shanks and the larger ER25 has a range of 1-16mm. Most router cutter sizes are the size of the shank i.e. a 5mm router cutter usually has a 5mm shank. This isn't the case with smaller cutters of 1mm diameter where a 1/8" (3.2mm) shank will often be used. Where possible it is better to have an interchangeable collet system on the router motor than a fixed one size collet found on small desktop machines – e.g. 1/8". I have both metric and imperial sized collets - it really depends on your preference.

Industrial machines have interchangeable tool systems - outside the scope of this book.

Fig 18: Router Collets

CNC Control System

The CNC has its own control system. Some CNCs come with their own proprietary controller, and often restrictive control system. Others, like mine, have an interface to link to various types of control systems.

My first CNC had a basic Chinese control system supplied with it free. This machine had a parallel cable port to link it to my computer with a free Chinese CAM program. This of course was at a time when parallel ports were disappearing from modern computers. I finished up having to buy an old second-hand computer with the legacy parallel port in order to get my CNC operating.

The CAD and control system packages supplied with my first CNC were so restrictive that I eventually replaced the control system with a new parallel interface card and linked it to Mach3 control system on my computer. An interesting experience! I learnt a lot about configuring CNC systems.

My new CNC has a modern controller with a USB connector to my Mach3 CNC control system package on my computer. I am not dependent on proprietary control package and I can select add-ons from the large number available to me in the Mach3 community.

Many of the desktop models have now a USB interface and often supply some basic free control system. A normal desktop or laptop computer can drive these machines using a standard USB lead.

The CNC control system has several functions. It controls the motors for the X Y Z axes. It controls the spindle, on-off and in some cases speed, it controls the homing limits for the X Y Z axes. It can also control extra items like edge finders and height gauges.

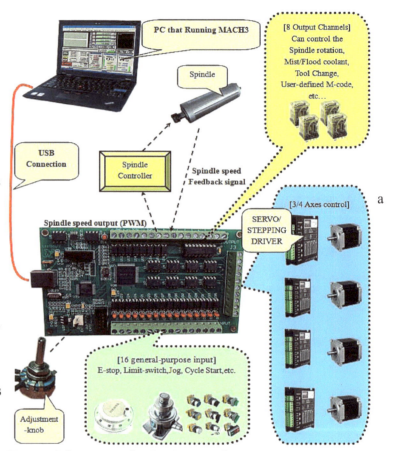

Fig 19: Schematic of a CNC control system

One great advantage of universal control system, like Mach3, is the wide range of add-ons and equipment that have been designed to work with it. I bought an add-on remote controller which enabled me to control my machine remotely - ideal when zeroing the axes and jogging the router cutter. Fig 20.

Fig 20: Remote Control

Router Cutters

Router cutters come in all shapes and sizes for different uses. There are straight flute cutters for general wood machining. There are spiral flute cutters for specialist machining where the cuttings need to be removed to avoid overheating (upward spiral), or the top needs to be compressed for machining like veneers and laminates (downward spiral).

There are V-cutters for engraving and round nosed cutters for carving. There are flat cutters for area clearance and roughing cutters for general material removal prior to the finishing cut. There are round-over cutters for creating a fillet. Fig 21.

Fig 21: Various Router Cutters

Basic router cutters used in furniture making are tungsten tipped. These brazed-on tips are not ideal for CNC routing as the tips can detach or the cutter breaks at the top of the tungsten tip with material fatigue caused by the huge forces exerted when the CNC router changes direction. I much prefer the router to be made from solid tungsten carbide. The solid carbide cutters are stronger, however they are more expensive.

The two critical dimensions are the diameter of the cutter and the depth of cut. It's no good using a 5mm diameter router cutter to mill a 3mm diameter hole. Likewise it's not very clever to use a 1mm diameter router cutter with a height of 5mm to cut out a 3m long bookshelf from 12.5mm thick material.

There are milling cutters that are designed to be used with CNC Milling machines at relatively low speeds - say 1,000 RPM. These cutters should never be used for router cutting as they are not balanced to handle speeds up to 25,000 RPM.

Hand-held routers can only cut in one direction - the router rotation against the direction of travel. But this is not the best direction for accurate cutting - especially wood. A modern CNC Router will allow the cut to be in the 'climb' direction (rotation with the direction of travel) as well as the conventional rotation against the direction of travel. When cutting wood for example this can make quite a difference - depending on the grain direction, a cleaner cut can be obtained by cutting with the direction of travel - climb.

When cutting veneers or plywood, then a downward spiral is preferred to push the grain down. A straight or upward spiral cutter would lift the grain of the veneer surface.

I machine a lot of acrylic plastic. Initially I had major problems with the router cutter getting blocked with molten plastic cuttings. I tried different cutting speeds and cooling the cutter with compressed air - to no avail. I then read about upward spiral cutters; I bought one and tried it. Excellent. No clogging, clean cut and the swarf removed from the cutter quickly. Works with 15,000 RPM speed and no need to cool the cutter. Melting acrylic plastic can also be caused by using extruded acrylic for machining. The best acrylic plastic for CNC machining is cast acrylic.

Design Software - CAD

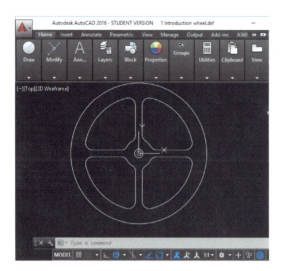

Fig 22: AutoCAD

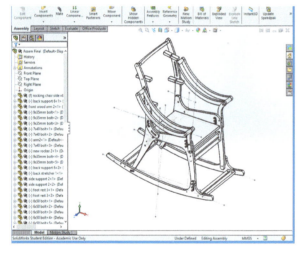

Fig 23: Solidworks rocking chair

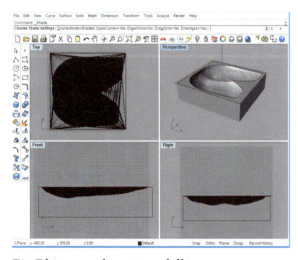

Fig Rhino mesh seat modelling

As I mentioned earlier there are three different software packages traditionally used together to operate a CNC Router.

1. Computer Aided Design software - CAD;

2. Computer Aided Manufacturing software - CAM

3. CNC machine control system.

Depending on what you have in mind making on your CNC will decide the software you need for design purposes. If like me, you plan to make items from plans published on the Internet, then there is no need to buy CAD software. Usually Internet designs are available in the standard interchange formats - DXF or STL, that can be read into most CAM packages.

There is a wide range of CAD software available, some free and some very expensive. For the Personal CNC user there are many free products with limited functionality but lack some of the more useful features found in industrial CAD software.

Industrial CAD packages depend on specific industries. For example in the furniture industry the standard package today is SOLIDWORKS (Fig 23) – it is designed to work the way a professional would work – that is starting from a solid piece of material and shaping it. There is a low cost sister product to SOLIDWORKS called DraftSight which has the basic CAD functions to get you started within an industrial framework.

Traditionally the market leading industrial package was AutoCAD (Fig 22) and today its DXF interchange format has become the industry standard. Any of these packages can be used for CAD design, but beware there is a steep learning curve with all of them. They rarely operate in the same way and knowledge of one is only of basic help when using another.

At University I used SOLIDWORKS extensively to design and build my flat-pack rocking chair. It enabled me to design each component separately and then assemble the components into an animated chair to ensure that they all worked together.

I also used Rhinoceros (Rhino) at University which is a very advanced 3D modelling package. Fig 24. Rhino is one of the leading exponents of modelling in mesh. I used this capability to take a scanned image of a chair seat, based on a mould of my bottom, and develop a 3D mesh that was used to program the CNC to cut out the chair seat.

A major area of consideration is the output of your design in either vectors or point-to-point stereo lithography (STL). Some CAM packages only work with STL files. The difference between the two types is that a vector output will render a smooth curve; a STL output will be a series of triangles joined together. This is the standard interface for 3D printers. Obviously the larger number of points will minimize the effect of the straight edges. This is further compounded by the CNC Control System, as some CNC control system products can only receive point-to-point commands and not handle vector curves and arcs. The big advantage of Mach3 control system is that it supports both types of input. So I can achieve beautiful arcs – not a series of dotted lines or triangles.

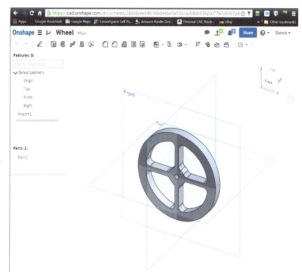

Fig 25: Solidworks 3D CAD representation

Using CAD software

There are hundreds of different CAD systems available - they perform very similar tasks but their operation may be completely different. I have only limited experience with one CAD system, so I am unable to offer any assistance on other CAD systems.

To give the reader an idea of how CAD software works I have constructed the following example using a very simple wheel design.

This wheel design will enable most readers to set up in their CAD system.

Fig 26. Basic CAD Setup

To start with I created 4 circles from a common centre point. The outer will be the wheel rim, the next will be the wheel rim thickness, the third will be the wheel axle and the fourth will be the centre hole to run on the spindle. The sizes I have chosen are 100mm rim x 10mm thickness and 20mm axle with a 5mm spindle hole. As per the diagram opposite.

Using the dimension tool I have annotated the dimensions on the drawing.

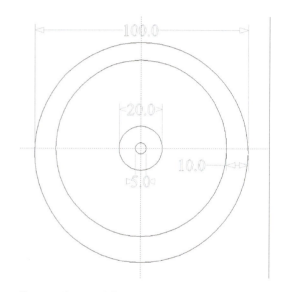

Fig 26: Basic CAD Setup

Fig 27. Construct the spokes

To create the spokes I have constructed rectangles horizontally and vertically to touch the spindle hole at a tangent. The CAD system I am using allows me to snap onto the inner rim circle and the centre spindle hole. The lines have to meet or overlap these vectors to ensure that the completed design does not have any gaps.

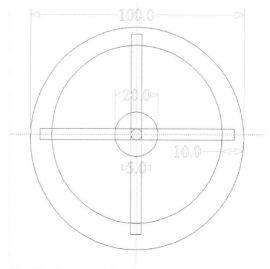

Fig 27: Construct Spokes

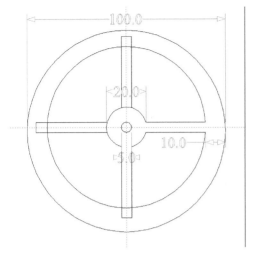

Fig 28. Trim the Spokes

Using the 'Trim' tool I now trim away the unwanted parts of the drawing - like a very accurate eraser. You have to be careful you leave the parts that are needed. I luckily have a 'back' button which allows me to backtrack or start again when I make mistakes.

Fig 28. Trim the Spokes

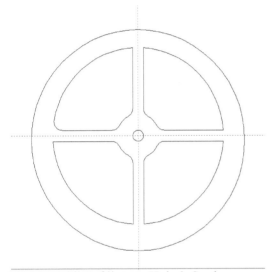

Fig 29 Adding fillets to Hub & Spoke

To finish off the design I will add fillets to all the internal corners. I have used a 5mm radius fillet which my router bit will be able to follow without any trouble.

Fig 29: Adding fillets to Hub & Spoke

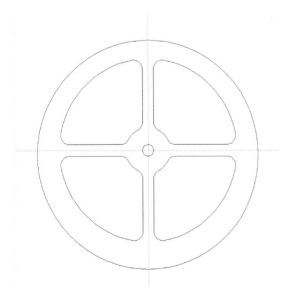

Fig 30: Completed hub and spoke

The sketch is now complete and can be exported to the CAM package. My CAM package has various import formats but as already mentioned the AutoCAD dxf file works well for vectors.

Obviously CAD packages allow the user to undertake lots of tasks - this is just a simple example of how CAD systems work.

Fig 30: Completed hub and spoke

Most CAD packages are supplied with tutorials which I strongly recommend you work through. Its surprising how you can waste such a lot of time trying to move to the next stage of a drawing when you don't know the simple short-cuts. I also bought instruction manuals for my CAD software. These act as a quick cross-reference when trying to understand how to do specific tasks.

As I mentioned before, I have used 4 different CAD packages Solidworks, OnShape, Rhino and AutoCAD, but only one fully Solidworks . They all work very differently. Its only with constant use that the brain automatically remembers how to undertake the short-cuts - especially when the brain starts to fail in old age like mine!

A friend of mine, similarly old-aged, has also tried three different CAD packages without avail - never spending enough time to really understand the package before trying another. Its important that when you find one you stick with it and really get to know it by working through various examples. You will never become competent with the package by just reading the text-book - you have to persevere by using the package. It's the little obvious tasks that take the time to pick up - I have often stared at the package for ages trying to figure out how to perform a simple task. But once you know the package stick with it - the grass on the other side is always greener but these packages are all very different and take a lot of time to get to know properly.

Having explained all of this I cannot stress how modern CAM packages are now so comprehensive you may not need a stand-alone CAD package at all.

In a recent Google search it found over 42 million CAD packages listed! Fig 31.

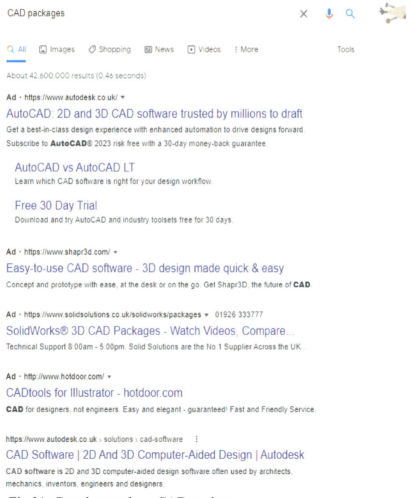

Fig 31: Google search on CAD packages

CAM Software

This has historically been the domain of Engineers. Its only in the last few years that these packages have tried to integrate both CAD and CAM for designer makers and hobbyists like me. There are free CAM packages as well as industrial versions costing over $10,000.

Having tried several I prefer to use a general purpose package from Vectric called Cut2D which is low cost and ideal for hobby use. Vectric has more advanced 3D packages but I only needed the 2D version. Vectric has an excellent support forum and tutorials as well as many add-ons to extend the capability of the package. In the early days I used an entry level CAM package from Delcam called ArtCAM. It's no longer available from the developer after being taken over by AutoDesk. There are still pirate copies available - not recommended,

Overview (CAM)

The CAM package allows the operator to decide how the item is going to be machined. In Industry, the CAD systems are used by designers and the CAM systems by engineers. Thankfully there are some packages that are breaking down these barriers and allow the design process to be accomplished in the CAM system - like Vectric.

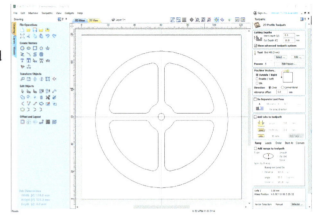

Fig 32: Vectric Cut2D

The basic functions of a CAM package are:-

1. Selection of the tools to be used in the machining.
2. The path the tool will take - outside, along or inside the vector
3. The dimensions of the material
4. The depth of cut
5. The cutting characteristics of the tool
6. Generating the output toolpath in machine code.

Most CAM packages will have a tool database where the characteristic for the tools to be used for machining are stored. This database usually records the following information:-

1. Type of material to be cut - hardwood, plastic.
2. Imperial or Metric tools
3. Type of tool - Ball Nose, V-bit, End Mill, Engraving etc.
4. Diameter of the tool
5. Cutting parameters
6. Spindle speed - the router spindle speed
7. Feed rate - the speed the tool cuts the material - X,Y direction
8. Plunge rate - the speed the tool drills down - Z direction

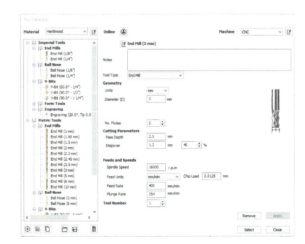

Fig 33: Vectric Cut2D Tool Database

The design from the CAD package is transferred to the CAM package in a digital format. The most common is AutoCADs Digital Exchange Format (dxf). This is a vector driven format so curves are depicted by arcs and not individual points. During the import of the design the CAM package will require the dimensions of the material to be machined.

The CAM package lets me to specify the start reference position for the material. I usually make the start position the top of the material in the bottom left hand corner. But for circular items I will often select the top centre of the material.

Once the toolpaths are configured in the CAM package they are then converted by the 'Post Processor' built into the CAM package to turn the DXF file into G-Code. There are many variations in G-Code dependent on the control system of the CNC. Vectric supports hundreds of different outputs.

Using CAM software

To explain the operation of a typical CAM software package I will take you through the steps to configure the wheel we developed in CAD for machining.

On loading the dxf file into the CAM system, Cut2D asks for the size of the material to be machined. It has already worked out the size from the dxf file but you may want to alter this if you are using a larger piece of material. It is also asks for the job origin - I have specified the bottom LH corner.

Before the toolpaths are determined the thickness of the material is set up. The wheel is designed for 10mm thick acrylic so 10mm has been selected as the thickness. This screen also confirms that I want the starting point to be in the LH corner of the top of the material. There are options for the bottom as well.

The first tool path to be constructed is for the centre hole. This could be drilled with a 5mm drill or machined round with a 3mm mill. I prefer wherever possible to use the same router bit for the whole piece instead of having to change the tool mid-way though. This cannot always be achieved but in this example it can.

My CNC is very accurate and it can cut holes very well. On some CNCs that may not be the case. The first CNC I bought was particularly bad at cutting holes - backlash - they always turned out oval! So you may have to opt to use a twist drill to accurately cut holes if your machine has a backlash problem.

A 3mm diameter end-mill has been selected with the following characteristics:-

Finish depth	10.2mm
Pass Depth	2.5mm
Stepover	1.2mm
Feed rate	400 mm/min
Plunge rate	254 mm/min
Spindle speed	16,000 rpm

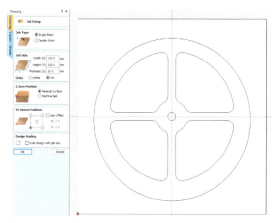

Fig 34: Vectric Cut2D Material setup

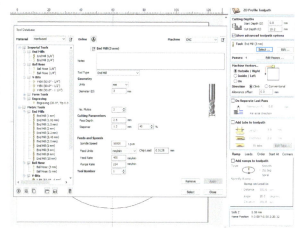

Fig 35: Detailing the tool requirements

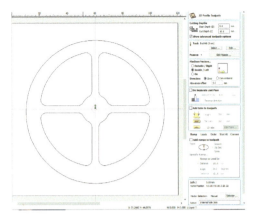

Fig 36: Toolpath for the centre-hole

A finished depth of 10.2 has been set to ensure the end-mill cuts through the material and leaves a clean edge on the underside. It will be cutting 0.2mm into the sacrificial baseboard which is not a problem and will give a clean cut on the underside. The hole vector is selected and the toolpath calculated. Fig 36.

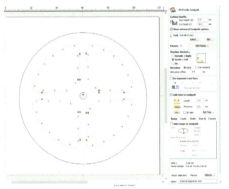

Fig 37: Toolpath and tabs for internal segments

The next toolpath will cut out the inner segments for the spokes. The 3mm diameter end-mill is selected again using the same parameters. But this time we want to add tabs to stop the cut-out sections flying off and damaging the piece. I have specified 2 tabs of length 3mm and 2mm thickness. I have positioned them on the straight sections as they will be easier to clean up afterwards. Fig 37.

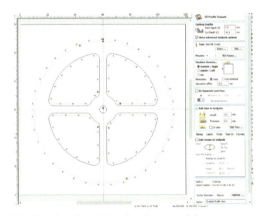

Fig 38: Toolpath with tabs for outside

The final toolpath is the outer rim. Again the 3mm diameter end-mill has been selected. The outer vector has been selected. Two tabs have been added to control the piece while machining and the toolpath saved. Fig 38.

Before outputting the G-Code I have specified the safe working height for my router - a height that will allow it to be repositioned without colliding with anything. In this case 5mm.

I usually save the individual toolpaths with a brief explanation in the description of which toolpath this is and the size of router needed. e.g. 'Outside Profile 3mm'.

The toolpaths are now converted into G-Code by the CAD Post Processor system. In my case the machine file output has been specified as Mach3 MM Arcs. Yours may be different. The output will be a txt file - there are options to save the toolpaths separately and to append the tool size to each file. The file is saved in a specified directory where it can be selected by the CNC control system - in my case a directory named 'toolpaths'. When saving the toolpaths it also allows me to put a title suffix on each toolpath showing which project its for e.g. 'Wheel _1-Outside Profile 3mm' Fig 39.

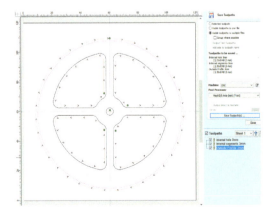

Fig 39: Completed toolpaths ready for saving

CNC Control System

There are basically five functions of the control system:

The tool selected for machining.
The feed rate of that tool for different materials
The speed of the router spindle.
The start position on the material.
Reading and interpreting the G-Code input.

Many CAD packages let you specify these elements but it's important to discuss them at this stage.

As I mentioned earlier, many CNC manufacturers have their own control systems which due to their wide diversity cannot be discussed here. At University the CNC Router had its own control console which was so complicated only the technician could use it. See Fig 40. When I bought my first CNC it came with a free

Fig 40: Industrial CNC with proprietary controller

Chinese control system package to operate the CNC. The connection to the computer was with a parallel cable with only limited functionality. To set it up I had to buy a second-hand computer with a parallel port as modern computers no longer supported parallel interfaces. The control system operating manual was a very basic translation from the Chinese - a lot was lost in the translation.

I decided to update the control system to Mach3. I purchased a new control card which also used a parallel cable and rewired my machine. I learnt a lot about the operation on the CNC and was delighted to get it fully operational. The parallel cable limited the range of signals that could be sent. I only had three speed settings for my router spindle. So I rewired an external potentiometer to the Router Spindle's Inverter so that I had a variable speed control for the spindle - with the control system only switching it off and on.

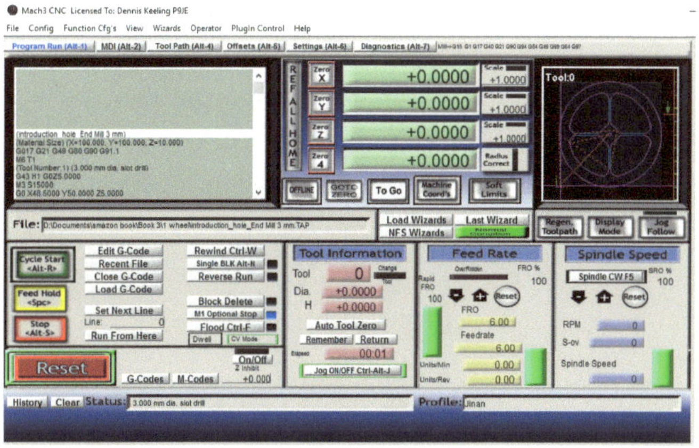

When specifying the configuration of my replacement CNC I wanted to make use of Mach3's recent capability to use a USB interface with a very wide range of configurable ports available - like variable spindle speed control. What a difference this made. Parallel cables are old technology that has now been replaced by USB. Fig 41.

Fig 41: Mach3 Control Panel on my PC

So for this book I am using Mach3 control system as a typical example of how control software operates. This is a general purpose system package that is extensively used in the industry on a wide range of different CNC machines. It is relatively cheap to purchase and has an excellent series of online tutorial videos as well as a popular support forum. Mach3 is very comprehensive, I will only be covering it's basic attributes in this book.

Fig 42: Mach3 compatible remote controller

I purchased a compatible remote controller as well as specialist software to machine gears. Fig 42.

Tool selection

Since I do not have an automatic tool changer I try to use the same router bit for the whole job to save the trouble having to change the cutter and reset the starting height each time. There may be exceptions to this when a small diameter router is needed for accurate finishing of gear teeth or when a larger router is needed for roughing long runs. This means specify the tool information in the CAM package, as already discussed.

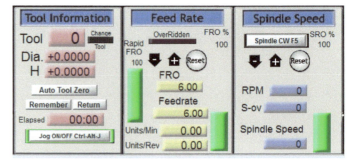

Fig 43: Mach 3 Control Panel

Feed rate

The size of the router will also govern the speed of machining. For example selecting a 3mm diameter 10mm height slot mill will be slower to machine than say a 10mm diameter cutter but much faster than a 1mm diameter cutter.

The feed rate is the speed the router travels over the material. The feed rate is related to the size of the router; its speed; the number of cutting edges; the depth of cut and the material to be machined. This is a formula published by AXYZ International.

Feed rate is calculated using the following equation:

Feed = N x cpt x RPM

N - number of cutting edges (flutes)

cpt - chip load (chip per tooth) is the amount of material, which should be removed by each tooth of the cutter as it rotates and advances into the work. (mm per tooth)

RPM - the speed at which the cutter revolves in the spindle. (Revolutions per minute)

If you are running at 18000 RPM using a 25mm end-mill with two flutes, and a recommended chip load of 0.1 mm/tooth:

Feed = 2 x 0.1 x 18000 = 3600 mm per min

The calculation can be quite complex and many router bit manufacturers publish recommended charts for their tools - see Amana Tool opposite. Fig 44.

For a straight cut with an 8mm router with two flutes I would use a 1,000 mm/min feed rate. For a simple wheel design in Acrylic Plastic material using a 3mm router bit I would use a 500mm/min feed rate. But that is personal choice on the type of material to be machined, the size of the tool and the capability of the router motor. If during machining you feel that the feed rate is either too fast or too slow, the feed rate can be overridden in the Mach3 Control Panel.

Solid Carbide Plastic Cutting Spiral Single 'O' Flute Router Bits

Diameter	IPM at 18,000 RPM (Inches Per Minute)	Spindle Speed SFM (Surface Feet Per Minute)	Chip Load Per Tooth
1/16" (0.0625)	35 - 70	500 - 1,200	0.002" - 0.004"
2mm	35 - 70	500 - 1,200	0.002" - 0.004"
3/32" (0.0938)	55 - 90	500 - 1,200	0.003" - 0.005"
3mm	70 - 110	500 - 1,200	0.004" - 0.006"
1/8" (0.125)	70 - 110	500 - 1,200	0.004" - 0.006"
5/32" (0.1563)	110 - 145	500 - 1,200	0.006" - 0.008"
4mm	110 - 145	500 - 1,200	0.006" - 0.008"
3/16" (0.1875)	110 - 145	500 - 1,200	0.006" - 0.008"
5mm	110 - 145	500 - 1,200	0.006" - 0.008"
6mm	145 - 220	500 - 1,200	0.008" - 0.012"
1/4" (0.250)	145 - 220	500 - 1,200	0.008" - 0.012"
9/32" (0.2813)	145 - 220	500 - 1,200	0.008" - 0.012"
5/16" (0.3125)	160 - 235	500 - 1,200	0.009" - 0.013"
8mm	160 - 235	500 - 1,200	0.009" - 0.013"
21/64" (0.3281)	180 - 250	500 - 1,200	0.010" - 0.014"
11/32" (0.3438)	180 - 250	500 - 1,200	0.010" - 0.014"
9mm	200 - 290	500 - 1,200	0.011" - 0.016"
3/8" (0.375)	200 - 290	500 - 1,200	0.011" - 0.016"
10mm	200 - 290	500 - 1,200	0.011" - 0.016"
12mm	270 - 360	500 - 1,200	0.015" - 0.020"
1/2" (0.250)	270 - 360	500 - 1,200	0.015" - 0.020"

Tool Reference #'s

Up-Cut	Down-Cut	Dia.
51403	—	1/4"
51404	51504	1/4"
51405	51505	1/4"
51407	51507	1/4"
51409	—	1/4"
51410	51510	1/8"
51411	51511	1/8"
51412	51512	3/16"
51413	51513	1/4"
51414	51514	3/8"
51415	51515	1/16"
51416	—	1/8"
51417	51517	3/16"
51418	—	1/4"
51419	—	1/4"
51421	51524	1/4"
51424	—	7/32"
51425	—	1/4"
51426	51509	3/8"
51427	—	3/8"
51428	—	1/2"
51429	—	3/8"
51441	—	1/16"
51442	—	3/16"
51443	—	1/8"
51444	—	1/4"
51445	—	1/8"
51446	—	1/8"
51447	51516	5/32"
51448	51518	3/16"
51449	—	3/16"
51453	—	1/4"
51491	—	3mm
51493	—	5mm
51495	—	6mm
51497	—	6mm
51499	—	6mm
—	51519	1/4"
51634	—	2mm
51636	—	4mm
51638	—	6mm
51643	—	3/8"
51644	—	1/2"

Simple Machining Calculations:
To find **RPM:** (SFM x 3.82) / diameter of tool
To find **SFM:** 0.262 x diameter of tool x RPM
To find **Feed Rate:** RPM x # of flutes x chip load
To find **Chip Load:** IPM / (RPM x # of Flutes)

Depth of Cut: 1 x D Use recommended chip load
2 x D Reduce chip load by 25%
3 x D Reduce chip load by 50%

Fig 44: Amana Tool feed rate table

Spindle speed

The spindle speed will depend on the size of the router cutter, the range of the router motor and the type of material to be machined. In the last example I was machining Acrylic Plastic so that needs a slower speed than say plywood. My router motor has a range of 200 – 25,000 rpm. Again the spindle speed can be adjusted during machining without stopping the job.

Opposite is a table published by ShopBotTools USA, which gives some typical values. Fig 45

The tool database supplied with the CAM system enables the characteristics of each tool to be stored and edited if necessary. Vectric provides an extensive tool database with these parameters already worked out for each choice of tool. Its very rare that I have to edit its database suggestion.

Soft wood

Name	SB#	Onsrud Series	Cut	Chip Load per leading edge	Flutes	Feed Rate (ips)	Feed rate (ipm)	RPM	Max Cut
1" 60 degree Carbide V cutter	13648	37-82	1 x D	.004-.006	2	2.4-3.6		18,000	
1/4" Straight V Carbide Tipped End Mill	13642	48-005	n/a	n/a	1	n/a	n/a	n/a	
1/2" Straight V Carbide Tipped End Mill	13564	48-072	n/a	n/a	2	n/a	n/a	n/a	
1/4" Upcut Carbide End Mill	13528	52-910	1 x D	.007-.009	2	4.2-5.4		18,000	
1/4" Downcut Carbide End Mill	13507	57-910	1 x D	.007-.009	2	4.2-5.4		18,000	
1/4" Upcut Carbide End Mill	1108	65-025	1 x D	.004-.006	1	1.2-1.8		18,000	
1/8" Tapered Carbide Upcut Ball End Mill	13636	77-102	1 x D	.003-.005	2	1.8-3.0		18,000	
1-1/4" Carbide Tipped Surfacing Cutter	13555	91-000	1/2-3/4 x D		2		200-600	12,000-16,000	1/8"

Fig 45: Typical spindle speeds - ShopBotTools

Configuring the CNC

Most CNCs will be delivered with their configuration set up in the control system. Unfortunately the early machines I purchased directly from China didn't and I had to set everything up myself.

Mach3 gives very clear tutorials and videos on how to configure Mach3 for your CNC. The main elements are:-

1. Configuring the units of measure - metric or imperial

2. Configuring the inputs and outputs

3. Tuning the stepping and spindle motors

4. Setting the machine co-ordinates.

5. Axis calibration

The recent CNC machines I have bought had all of these set up which is a dream!

The configuration will depend on interface board being used in the CNC. The screen shots opposite show the typical configuration of the Motor Outputs, the Input Signals. Sometimes the XYZ home indicators as well as the limits are output from sensors on those axes.

Each stepping motor is then configured in terms of steps, velocity and acceleration. This information is usually supplied with the stepping motor. Each axis has top be set up separately as well as the spindle motor. Fig 48.

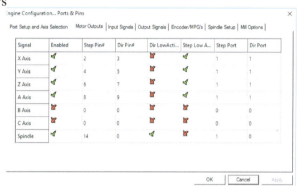

Fig 46: Mach3 Axes

Fig 47: Mach3 Outputs

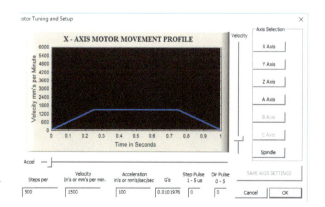

Fig 48: Mach3 Motor tuning

The CNC bed size is also configured in the control system. This enables the system to accurately predict the position of the router. It constantly keeps track on the machine co-ordinates. My machine has switches at the home positions for all three axes so the machine can be 'homed' to zero to reset the machine co-ordinates. Fig 49.

Fig 49: Mach3 Home limits

The starting position for machining does not have to be the hole position. Mach3 has a second set of co-ordinates which in-turn are zeroed to the starting point of the work. It also has the ability to specify off-sets to help with advanced setting out of the work. These offsets can be used for edge finders and also depth probes.

It is also worth checking the distance travelled. Mach3 allows me to set a distance travelled in each axis to check the accuracy. I usually use a 1m metal rule and set the distance to say 50cm from a start position. If the distance travelled is not quite 50cm then the actual distance travelled can be entered and Mach3 will recalculate the stepping size and update the configuration. Fig50.

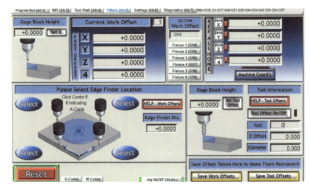

Fig 50: Mach3 Distance travelled

Having set up the control system, a sample G-Code project can be set up to check the operation.

Operating the CNC

The G-Code file is loaded into the CNC control system. Mach3 undertakes an initial check on the file to ensure its readable. It displays the toolpaths on the screen and you can see from the first two lines the G-Code is specifying the tool size and the material size. Fig 51.

The toolpaths are shown on the screen - the red dotted lines show the jogging at a safe height, the purple toolpaths the cutting and the blue toolpaths showing where the tabs will be created.

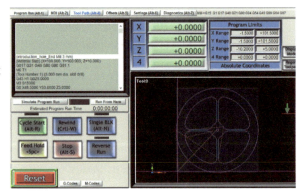

Fig 51: Mach 3 toolpaths

I have selected a 3mm diameter end-mill for the machining. An end mill is a general purpose router bit that can be used for drilling as well as slot cutting and area clearance. I could have used a 5mm end-mill which would still have been suitable for machining the 5mm fillets of the spokes as well as drilling the hole.

The type of router that I have used is a upward spiral solid tungsten carbide bit. The upward spiral is ideal for machining acrylics. It removes the chips quickly and therefore does not allow it to build up heat, melt and clog the router. Fig 52.

The router bit is held securely in the router usually by a collet chuck. My current router uses ER16 collets. The collets are slightly adjustable for example the 5mm collet has a range

Fig 52: Twin flute up-cut tungsten router mill

of 4mm - 5mm. A 5mm collet is not happy holding a 4mm bit. Most router bits shank size is the same size as the cutting diameter - there are exceptions of course but if you want to work with routers over a specific range then you should have exact size collets to fit them. So I have the whole set of collets from 1mm to 16mm in 1mm increments as well as 1/8" to 1" imperial sizes.

The smaller collet sizes have a holding area in the bottom third of the collet. The larger collets have a holding area the full length of the collet. Some router bits have a line to show the position of the router with respect to the collet holder. The general rule is only the round part of the shank (the section without any machined slot) should be in the collet.

One of my collet chucks has a flat nut to be tightened by a spanner. The other uses a Tommy bar and a special slotted tool to tighten up the collet. Most collets have a fail-safe hold on the collets to ensure that they don't become loose by accident. When removing the bit, the collet has to be loosened several turns to free the bit from the fail safe. Fig 53.

Fig 53: Tightening the Collet Nut

Fixing the material

The material to be machined has to be fixed to the base board. This will depend on the method of fixing the material to your CNC bed. As I mentioned before I always use a piece of MDF as a sacrificial base-board. This protects the actual base of my CNC and also allows me to over-cut into the baseboard in order to get clean edges on the underside.

For those with a metal slotted baseboard and clamps I would still use a piece of MDF as opposite with the miniature desktop CNC I used. Fig 54.

Fig 54: Metal slot fixing

My vacuum table is strong enough to hold large pieces of material but small pieces have to be secured to the base board using a glue gun. The forces exerted by the router when machining are considerable - especially when it changes direction, so the material has to be securely fastened. I use a hot-melt glue gun to secure the material to be machined to the MDF sacrificial bed. Fig 55.

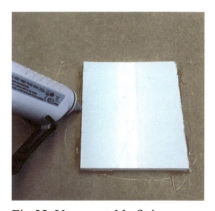

Fig 55: Vacuum table fixing

Starting position

The end-mill has been loaded into the collet chuck and the router spindle is jogged to the starting point - the top of the material in the bottom left hand corner. I have a remote controller which lets me set up the CNC using this device. My new CNC has a remote depth gauge which allows the start height to be accurately fixed.

Care should be taken finding the top of the material. A very good indicator is to use a thin piece of paper under the tool at the starting point. When the paper grabs its too far and the z axis is backed off until the paper can just move. There is no need to allow for the thickness of the paper - it is thin enough to not upset the zero. Fig 56

All three axes are now set to zero. It is always good practice to jog the router bit off the material to say a height of 5mm before starting machining.

Fig 56: Setting the start height and position

Machining with the CNC

We are ready to start machining.

The G-Code file is loaded, Mach3 does an initial check to ensure it's readable, then the system is set to Run. Fig 57.

The router will move to a safe height and jog to the first cutting point. The program first of all cuts the hole, it then jogs to the first internal segment then cuts the four internal segments. The router bit rises and falls around each tab leaving a fillet of material to hold the segments in place.

It then jogs to the outer rim and machines that. Since the material is 10mm thick it will not machine the whole depth on the first pass. The router has been programmed for a step-down of 2.5mm. So it will make at least four cuts around the outer tool path. Again it will be rising and falling around the tabs. When machining has finished the router will reposition itself at XY zero and the safe height for Z.

Fig 57: Ready to start machining

The tabs are cut though using an oscillating saw - try not to catch the finished material with the saw blade.Fig 58.

The tabs are then removed and cleaned up with a warding file on the vice.

Fig 58: Tabs cut

Engraving

One of the most popular uses of the small CNC Router is for Engraving. The majority of the desk-top CNC Routers on sale are used for Engraving purposes. The first project I undertook on my CNC was to engrave my name. Fig 59.

Engraving on the CNC is a simple and straightforward task. It doesn't need an expensive CNC to undertake the work a small router motor spindle will usually work well.

Opposite is a clock dial I engraved using a small inexpensive desktop CNC. Fig 60.

Engraving can be undertaken by using a slot router bit or a pointed router bit. The slot (round) router bit tracing a centre line will not machine the sharp corners found on most type faces (serif) - it leaves a rounded look. Whereas the pointed router bit and an engraving option in the CAD package will cut the sharp serifs and corners. I docs this by introducing a V cut at the top of each stroke. See lower example on the letter K below.

Engraving fonts

Most CAD and CAM packages allow you to define text. But one thing to be careful of is the choice of font - has it been designed for vectors? My first attempt at engraving text was a disaster for two reasons. The first was the choice of font and the second was the choice of the engraving tool for that font - Fig 61.

My CAM package had a wide range of fonts available. I chose a True Type font. But the subsequent tool path was awful - see below.

The tool paths were split and badly formed. I then realised my mistake and chose a vector engraving font.

This has clean tool paths and the characteristic 'v' at the end of each letter.

Fig 59: Engraving your name

Fig 60: Engraving a clock dial

Fig 61: Early engraving mistakes

Engraving Router Bits

Lettering is best undertaken with a V shaped pointed router bit. They come in various sizes - opposite is a 3mm diameter V Bit and also a 25mm diameter V-bit. The V can be anything from 60° to 150°. There are also v-shaped router bits with a spade end which are used for chamfering. They are not suitable for engraving- see picture below. It was this type of bit that I used for the bad engraving example shown on the previous page.

Engraving material

A wide range of materials can be engraved - from stone to plastics. For sign making I used a special sign-making engraving laminate sheet which is a sandwich of a darker material between two outer lighter coloured sheets. In my case I used a white outer and a 3mm thick black inner. The outers are usually protected by a film of polythene which protects the surface from scratching and can be peeled off later. These laminate sheets are available in a wide range of colours, thickness's and sheet sizes.

For a project I undertook for the Good Woodworking magazine I engraved my wife's name on the white plastic lid of the Jewellry Box. See below.

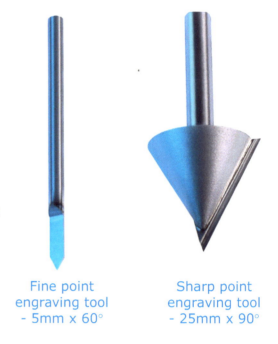

Fine point engraving tool - 5mm x 60°   Sharp point engraving tool - 25mm x 90°

Incorrect bit. V shaped chamfer bit - not suitable for engraving.

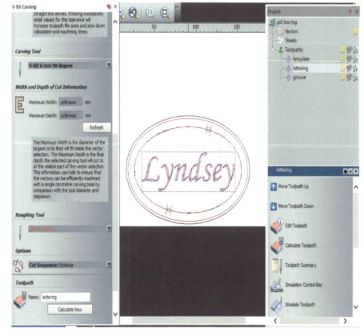

Fig 62: Setting up a Carving in ArtCAM

Fig 63: The completed jewellry box

Carving

Machining a 3D Relief

One of the most popular uses of the Personal CNC Router is for carving. It is this process that has spurred on the rapid use of these excellent machines. Most CAD systems can develop 3D relief artwork. Machining a 3D relief is also used in furniture making - for example in the profiling of chair seats.

While I was taking my University course I was fascinated by the shaped profile of the seat of the Windsor Chair - Fig 64. My research showed that there was in fact very little science behind the design of the sculptured seat. It had been developed through trial and error using quite primitive woodworking tools like the Adze. Traditional Windsor Chair makers use a specialised machine called the Adzder to profile the Elm seats. Today most of the Windsor Chair seats are cut using a CNC Router - but based on what shape of bottom? A British Standard Seat was designed - which didn't seem very comfortable to me.

So I decided to make a mould of my own bottom, have the mould scanned and digitised, and then use the scanned image to program the CNC. As I mentioned earlier, I used a CAD program called Rhinoceros (Rhino) for its ability to use mesh technology for the solid shape, to create the rendered output. Fig 65. Then the output was carved on the Uni's CNC. Fig 66.

The big disappointment to me was how long it takes to machine a carving. It looks so simple but when you get into the CAM design you realise it needs hundreds of repetitive cuts to machine a relief. The machining is undertaken by ball-nose or rounded CNC carving bits. Some have a circular shape others a tapered shape - to give a smoother finish.

Fig 64: Windsor chair with sculptured seat

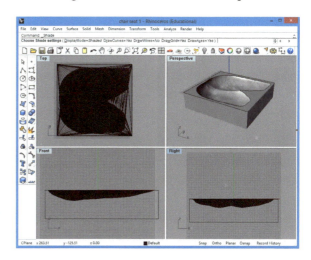

Fig 65: Digitised seat shape

Fig 66: CNC machined seat

The path that the CNC takes to cut the design can vary considerably between CAM packages. My old ArtCAM Express package, opposite, has an option for machine relief (carving) and lets you choose between classic raster and raster X Y. Whereas another CAM program, DeskProto (Fig 67), provides a much wider range of machining options. A lot will depend on the sort of carving you wish to undertake and the accuracy of the result.

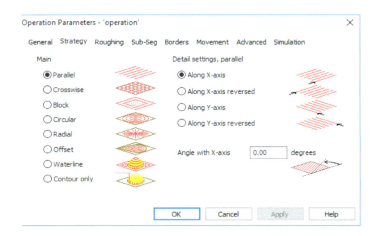

Fig 67: Deskproto relief selection

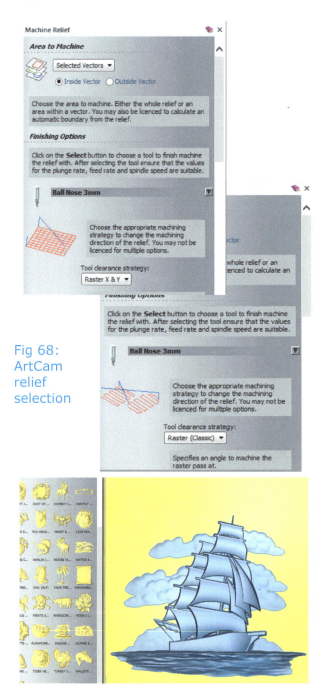

Fig 68: ArtCam relief selection

In my booklet entitled 'Personal CNC Routing, 10 Simple Projects' I cover in detail the machining of a wall plaque opposite as a carving project. The key stages are as follows:-

I used a standard relief from the library supplied with ArtCAM Express. Obviously you can develop your own relief or create a relief from a photograph, one of the options available in the CAD package. Fig 68.

This relief will be an embossed surface relief. Alternatively a negative relief can be created with the relief carved into the surface. In order to make the carving stand out I decided to leave a surround around the relief to show the original height of the material being carved.

Fig 69: ArtCAM standard images

Using ArtCAMs 'Create a machine relief' wizard, it allowed both a roughing and a finishing tool to be specified. In this case I used a 1/4" (6.3mm) ball nose spiral router for the roughing and a 4mm ball nose spiral router for the finishing. Fig 70.

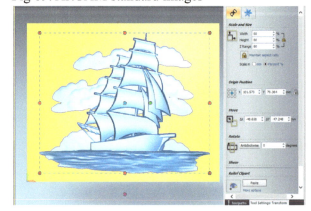

Fig 70: Designing the machining of the relief

The 1/4" spiral ball nosed router cutter is used for the roughing cuts. Fig 71.

By setting the step down higher than normal, 4.5mm, only 3 Z levels have to be machined to rough the 10mm depth.

Stepover   2.0mm
Stepdown   4.5mm
Feed rate   1500 mm/min
Plunge rate 400mm/min
Spindle Speed 15,000 rpm
Allowance 0.5 (for finishing)

Fig 71: Roughing cut

The finishing cut only cuts one level but profiles the whole relief going from 0 to -10mm Z movement.

The edge of the border is ragged from the raster cutting necessitating the cleaning up with a router following the rectangular border vector.

Stepover   0.4mm
Stepdown   3 mm
Feed rate   1,200 mm/min
Plunge rate 600 mm/min
Spindle speed 15,000 rpm
Allowance 0.0

Fig 72: Finishing cut

Fig 73: Completed relief

Furniture & Cabinetmaking

I suppose it was IKEA that really brought flat-pack furniture making to the fore. The ability to make furniture that could be so accurately machined that the end-user can self assemble the furniture. It saved on assembly, shipping, storage and of course delivery charges. Flat-pack furniture was the result of investment in CNC machining to high tolerances that could be repeated continuously. Fig 74.

In order to make flat-pack furniture that could be easily assembled and remain robust in use took some cleaver thinking in the way furniture was designed and made. Many of the tradition jointing methods would be difficult to machine. So new methods, using dowel barrel bolts, replaced conventional mortice and tenons and even dovetail joints. Traditional solid-wood panels were replaced by veneered MDF which would not warp, be of constant thickness and easily machined.

Fig 74: Ikea's influence on flat-pack furniture

Obviously modern furniture is now made from advanced CNC machinery that is not restricted to 2 or 3 axes like the hobbyist machines. Rotary and multi-axis machines can now machine the ends as well as around the item being machined. But that is outside the scope of this introductory booklet. We will concentrate on using the CNC for basic furniture and cabinet making applications. Fig 75.

Joining flat panels together can be simple, unfortunately we are hampered by the fact that the 3D CNC router cannot cut internal right-angles - there is always the shape of the router cutter to impede us - see below.

Fig 75: Multi-axis industrial machining

Router cutter

Wood to be machined

Simple overlap joint

There are of course ways that this can be resolved. In the simple Bird nestbox example in my other book 3, I minimised the effect of the fillet in the internal corner of the project by using a small diameter router cutter - 5mm and then manually filing the fillet away before assembly. (Fig 76). The design uses the push together mortice joint which is later secured with wood-screws.

This design relies of the stiffness of the 6.5mm birch plywood for its construction. Like all of these designs the accuracy of the machining is imperative. By designing the nest box in the CAM system, the dimensions can be standardised and depending on the accuracy of the CNC router the material can be machined accurately.

An allowance often has to be made when machining joints to ensure that they fit together. My CNC router is very accurate and I only made an allowance of 0.2 mm on the joint to enable ease of fitting. I am sorry to say its a bit of trail and error to get the allowance correct. In this case its not too important as the critical sections all have to be filed to remove the router cutter fillets. Fig 77.

Opposite is the finished bird box, covered in book 3, that is held together with small brass screws. Fig 78.

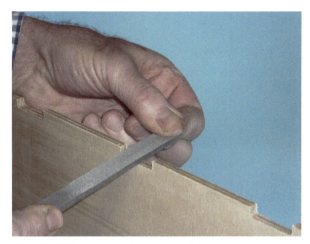

Fig 76: Filing away the corner fillet

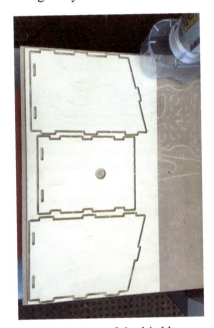

Fig 77: Design of the bird box

Fig 78: Completed bird box

Advanced slot (dog-bone)joint

With careful design the router can be used to cut back into the internal right angle to eliminate manual finishing. The cut-out for the router undercuts slightly the two sides but leaves the corner of the right angle in place to give the tightness of the joint. For this small item I used a 2mm router for the final profile cut. A small router gives a less obtrusive corner.

The drawing is constructed by first defining the internal shape of the slot. Then insert 45^0 construction lines from each corner. Draw circles, the size of the router bit +0.1mm, centred on the 45^0 line and cutting the corner intersection. Trim away the unwanted lines. Since the indents are slightly oversize the router will be able to make the cuts. Vectric Cut2D has a dog-bone fillet feature that creates these joints automatically - just select the cutter diameter. Fig 79.

The tenon that fits into the slot will be normal size and rectangular in shape. Opposite is a desk tidy I constructed using this method which is covered in the other book 3 of this series.

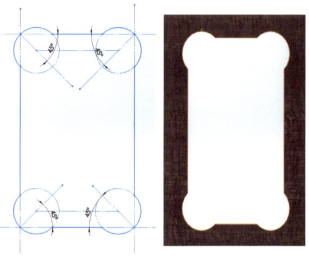

Fig 79: Designing a dog-bone corner

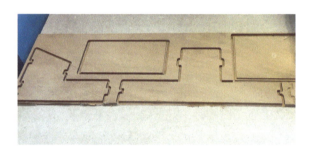

Fig 80: Desk-tidy built with dog-bone fillets

Traditional loose wedge mortice and tenon

The stool I constructed in Book 3 used the dog-bone joint shown above as well as the loose wedge joint for the stretcher. Fig 81. With this project I used a 5mm diameter router cutter, in order to machine 15mm plywood. The cut backs are hardly noticeable on the finished piece. Fig 82.

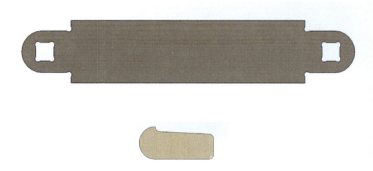

Fig 81: Dog-bone fillet stretcher with loose wedge joint

Fig 82: A stool designed with a wedge fillet stretcher

Cross-Dowel Barrel-Bolt construction

The cross-dowel barrel-bolt acts as a very strong means of joining sheets of material that may be subject to loads - like chairs. Dowels are available in various sizes from M4 onwards for various panel thickness's - 12mm onwards. Fig 83.

Fig 84: My rocking chair at Uni

Fig 83:
Barrel-Bolt

I first used them in the construction of my rocking chair at Uni to secure the stretchers to the side panels. Fig 84.

I also used them to secure the end panels to the drawers in my corner dressing unit for Good Woodworking magazine. Furniture makers use multi-axis CNC's to cut the dowel holes from the top and then the bolt holes from the side. For the hobbyist with a basic 2D CNC all we can cut are the dowel holes from the top with the CNC. The bolt holes have to be manually drilled very accurately. I had to ensure the side panels were held vertically to the drill bit - see picture below. Fig 85.

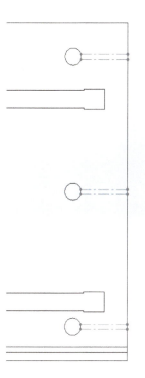

Fig 86: Designing barrel-bolt joints

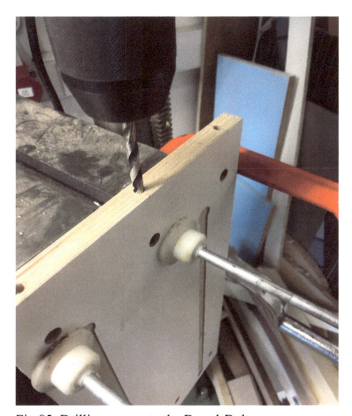

Fig 85: Drilling access to the Barrel-Bolt

Designing furniture

As I mentioned at the start of this book, *operating a CNC Router is simple - the skill is in creating a design that works and specifying the way it has to be machined.*

I admit that I am not an expert at designing a piece of furniture that works first time and looks good. I have been designing furniture for the Good Woodworking magazine and without exception all of my designs had to be changed before I felt they were right. You may be very lucky in having the ability to get the design right in CAD, getting the machining defined correctly in CAM and finally getting it machined correctly first time. I am not that person - for me there are too many variables that can all derail the project - and often do! The number of hiccups is proportional to ones age I have found.

Designing in CAD seems straightforward but I still find it hard to interpret a drawing into how it will actually look. I therefore tend to make a mock up from my design using cheap materials. It works out far cheaper that way than using expensive finished materials and having to scrap them. A classic example was the elegant coffee table I designed for Woodworking magazine see opposite. I wanted to make the top as large as possible on my old 600 x 600mm CNC table base. Fig 87.

I didn't make a mock-up but cut the table straight from the expensive melamine. What a monster table top! (Fig 88). I was luckily able to get away with it by re-machining the top - Fig 90, to get a much more aesthetically pleasing shape Fig 89.

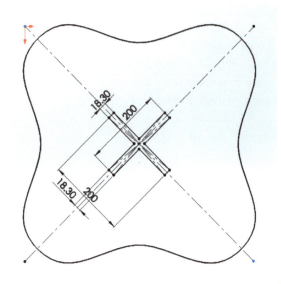

Fig 87: The original design in Solidworks

Fig 88: The completed first attempt

Fig 89: The streamlined finished table

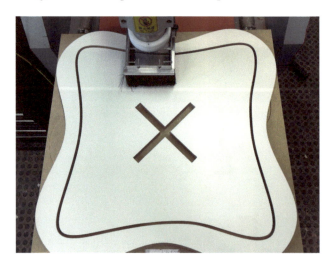

Fig 90: Reworking the top by securing the original.

All CAD packages are different. I use Solidworks which starts from a 3D solid. So I start with the overall shape of the component I am designing. I then add to this, as a separate stage, the extrusions or holes. I am able to accurately dimension the extrusion and holes and fix their position. Fig 91.

As I mentioned, I like to use curves, and CAD packages enable me to draw some beautiful curved shapes. Opposite you can see how I have shaped the legs of the table and on the previous page how I have shaped the table top. Curves are so easy to machine with a CNC but so difficult to produce with traditional woodworking methods.

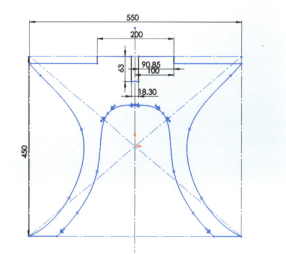

Fig 91: Plan of one side in Solidworks

It is very tempting to miss-out on the all important CAD assembly stage. I prefer to not only design the components of the piece I am making but also to assemble them in CAD to make sure the dimensions all work. The great thing about CAD is it is so precise to define measurements that can then be machined to very close tolerances. The table, (Fig 92) had all of it components created in CAD and then put together as an assembly to ensure it all worked. Pity I didn't spot the size of the top in proportion to the legs!

Unfortunately you have to persevere with CAD packages. They have an incredible number of options and work-abouts, only using the package in anger will enable you to really get to know it. Manuals and tutorials are great to get you started but there is nothing like trying to create your own piece of furniture.

Exporting to CAM

The CAD system I use does not directly integrate to my CAM system. So I have to save the output from CAD as a standard interchange file than can be read into my CAM system. Since I have developed the original design in vectors I want the interchange file to keep those vectors intact. Some interchange files save the vectors as a series of co-ordinates which can mean the beautiful shape of a vector is lost to a dotted line approximation.

Fig 92: 3D Assembled product in Solidworks

I have been using AutoCAD's dxf - Data Exchange Format. But be careful how the data is saved - I prefer to save using the 'faces/loops/edges' option (2D) as I have run into problems of distortion using the 'annotation views' option. Fig 93.

One of the gremlins that often occurs in the interface between CAD and CAM is lines from the drawing that are not fully joined. The slightest gap will stop my CAM system recognising an outline as a continuous vector loop.

Its also important to not export dimensions and construction lines specified in the CAD system to the CAM system, as this again confuses the CAM system.

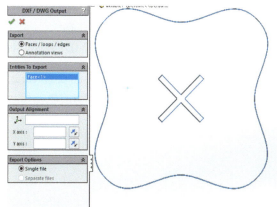

Fig 93: Exporting the dxf file to the CAM package

Using CAM

When choosing CAD, CAM and CNC control systems you have to make sure they all talk to each other easily. In my case they also all support vectors - I love to use smooth curves.

When starting a new project in Vectric Cut2D the first requirement is to select the overall dimensions of the material to be machined. Fig 94. My new CNC bed is 600 x 900 so I usually cannot exceed that size. I always allow the job-size to be oversize to ensure I can machine the item easily within it.

I set the zero position (X=0, Y=0, Z=0) at the datum point where the CNC router will be start. In this case I am using the top of the surface in the bottom left-hand corner. I very rarely change that setting otherwise it can introduce another variable to consider.

The Toolpaths are now defined. The CAM package usually lets you select from several types of toolpath. I usually use the 'Create Profile' toolpath for internal and external profiling. This toolpath has an option to follow the outside, inside or along the vector.

If I am cutting out a blind slot I would use the 'Create Area Clearance' toolpath. For drilling holes I would only use the drilling option if my router cutter was the same diameter as the hole I needed. Otherwise I would use the internal profile option to cut out any size hole that was larger than the router cutter.

When a toolpath type has been selected the details for that path are then set up. We will be machining from the top of the material downwards. So the start depth is 0.0 and the Cut Depth is 15.5mm. I am allowing 0.5mm over-cut to ensure a clean cut on the underside - this will cut into the sacrificial base-board, which in my case is usually 12mm MDF. (The vacuum works through the porous MDF base-board)

I usually start with the internal items requiring machining before the outside profile is cut. I also try, wherever possible, to use the same router bit for all the operations. However in this case I want to make a roughing cut with a 5mm router mill and a final cut with a 2mm router mill - to minimise the effect of the dog-bone fillet.

My system has options for allowances. I have allowed 1.0mm for the roughing cut that will be machined to the correct dimension by the final cut using the 2mm End Mill.

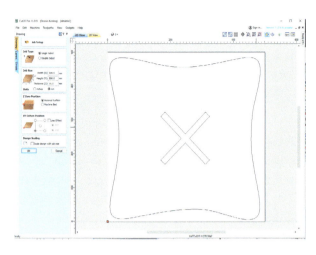

Fig 94: Vectric Cut2D material dimensions

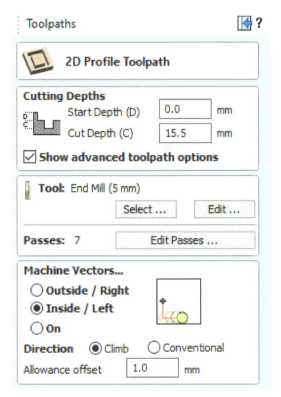

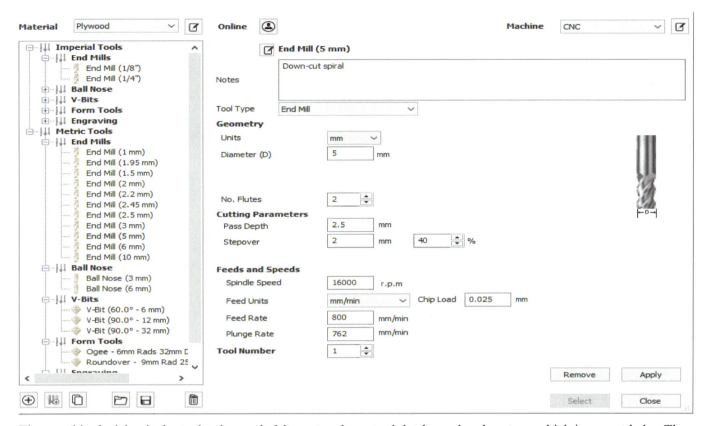

The next big decision is the tool to be used. My system has a tool database already set up, which is a great help. The database holds a typical selection of cutters for different materials and applications.

In this case we are cutting Plywood. So for plywood profiling it has a list of End Mill cutters from 1.0mm to 10mm in diameter with a down-cut spiral. Its important that the top surface of the plywood is protected from chipping so the spiral pushes the chips down initially.

The database holds separate information on each item. This can be overridden but in the main the database is very accurate. The main operating parameters are as follows:-

> Geometry
> > Diameter
> > Number of Flutes
>
> Cutting Parameters
> > Pass depth - stepdown
> > Stepover
>
> Feeds and Speeds
> > Spindle Speed
> > Chip load
> > Feed Rate
> > Plunge Rate

This is where the technical explanations should start, but this is not a workshop manual, and I won't try to explain the calculations of chip clearance - even if I did know how to calculate them.

I am an engineer by training and I have relied on trial and error in setting these variables, and as I have mentioned before, a lot will depend on your CNC, the material you are using and the router cutter.

Cutting different materials

The CNC Router can be used for cutting a wide range of materials. From solid wood, to plywood, to MDF and even to plastics and Corian. I even tried cutting metal but it wasn't successful as my CNC was not robust enough to handle the strain.

Cutting Wood

The traditional router cutter for wood is the tungsten-tipped straight router cutter. But I have found that the tungsten tips break off when CNC routing due to the rapid change of direction of the CNC. I prefer to use the solid carbide cutters. Solid Carbide cutters tend to be spiral in design. The spiral design creates some key attributes for routing.

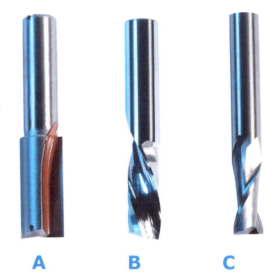

A   B   C

A. Straight tungsten-tipped router cutter

B. Downward spiral router cutter for laminates and veneers.

C. Upward spiral router cutter for rapid swarf removal

When cutting veneered plywood I would use a downward spiral router cutter which pushes the veneer downwards. I would also use the 'climb' (Down) cutting function which gives a much cleaner cut. Because the CNC can hold the material and the cutter head so securely it allows the climb cut to be achieved - this would be impossible to undertake with a hand-held router. Fig 95.

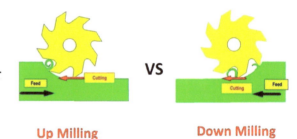

Up Milling   VS   Down Milling

Fig 95: The difference between Up and Down Milling

When planning to machine wood a lot of time can be saved by 'nesting' several components together and cutting them all at the same time. (Fig 96). Obviously the piece of wood being machined will dictate the nesting that can be accomplished. The machining of the planks of wood for the desk tidy, shown on the previous page, was limited by the size of the planks available. However the machining of the plywood stool below, took full advantage of the size of CNC bed.

The size of the router cutter will to a large part be dependent on the thickness of material. 15mm plywood will need a 1/4" or 6mm cutter to achieve the depth of cut. The cutting speed will in general be 15,000 RPM - higher speeds can be achieved on thinner material but always check the speed rating of the router cutter.

The feed rate will depend on what you are cutting. I use a low feed-rate for intricate work where the CNC cutter head is changing direction continuously. This avoids backlash - where the cutting head slightly overshoots on a change of direction. So I typically use 600 mm/min for intricate work and up to 1,500 mm/min for long straight runs like the stool opposite.

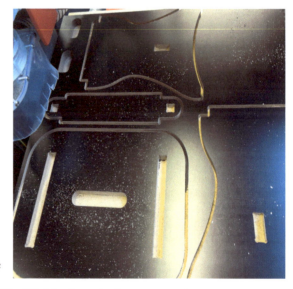

Fig 96: Nesting stool components

This book is not a workshop reference manual and I will not go into the science behind feed rates and cutting speeds (even if I did understand it). This is an introductory book for hobbyists and like me you will find out these things by trial and error. A lot will depend on the accuracy and robustness of your CNC. My first CNC was so bad that I constantly had to slow everything down and allow for its inaccuracies. My new machine, is very accurate and robust, so the speeds I can achieve my not be typical or suitable for your machine.

Fig 97: Cutting plastics

Cutting Plastics

Plastics like Acrylic, Perspex, Plexiglas, and Corian can easily melt when cutting and gum-up the router cutter. Slowing the speed down doesn't seem to make much difference. The secret is to use an upward spiral router cutter, which moves the material away quickly, and full extraction to cool the router bit. I cut a lot of plastic material; and I have no problems - I typically use 4 or 5mm router cutters at 15,000 rpm and a feed rate of 600 mm/min with full extraction on long runs.

Acrylic sheet comes in cast or extruded form. Extruded sheet quickly melts while machining whereas cast sheet machines well. Fig 97.

Tabs / Bridges

When defining a toolpath one has to consider what will happen to the piece once the external profile has been cut. In the case of the clock gear wheels above the last thing needed is for the router cutter to lift the gear wheel when completing the external profile and foul the gear teeth and damaging them. Even the vacuum table will not hold small items after machining.

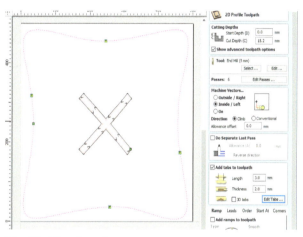

Fig 98: Simple tab setup

So most CAM systems have the ability to add tabs or bridges to the profile that act as hold-downs when the piece has been cut. In my system I can decide how many tabs to add, the length of the tab and the thickness. Fig 98. It suggests the positions for the tabs but I often re-position them to suit my requirements. I prefer to cut out the tabs afterwards with a oscillating saw so I would prefer the tab to be in a straight part of the profile. When cutting gear teeth, I prefer the tabs to be on the tips of the teeth.

Some systems will default on two tabs - one nearest the end point of the cutting and the other opposite that end point. For small items I will be happy with two tabs, but for larger items I prefer as many as four tabs.

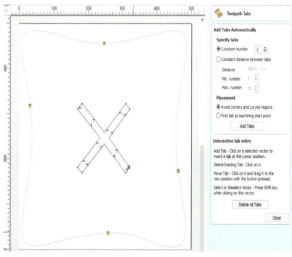

Fig 99: Advanced tab setup

Exporting the toolpaths

Once the various toolpaths have been specified they are then calculated in the Post Processor and exported in Machine-Code to the CNC Control System. My CAM system has a very wide range of export configurations to chose from for most of the most popular CNC machines in the world. It has a pull-down table to select the best configuration from. I use Mach3 as my CNC system and my CAM system gives me several options for Mach3. I chose the mm with arcs option. As I mentioned earlier I prefer to use vectors instead of point-to-point dotted lines and my CAM system allows me that option with Mach3.

The toolpaths are exported as either one big file or several files - one for each toolpath. For one-offs I prefer to have separate files so that if there is a mistake I can usually correct it before its too late. For long runs of proven code I would use the combined file. For Mach3 the G-Code is saved as a *.txt file You then have to get this code to the CNC System - in my case I save it to a USB stick and copy it into my CNC computer.

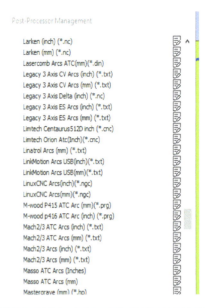

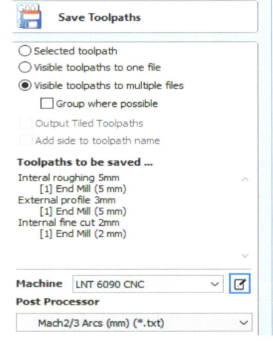

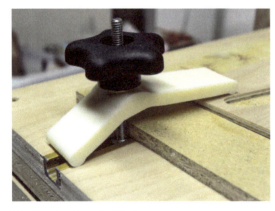

Fig Basic clam hold-down

Preparing the CNC for operation

The material has to be held securely for machining on the CNC. This can either be achieved using glue, other mechanical means, or a vacuum bed. The forces exerted by the router during machining are considerable so the means of securing the material has to be rigid and fit for the type of machining being undertaken.

The larger industrial router machines tend to use vacuum either as a vacuum table or as vacuum pods. The smaller desktop router machines would use either a baseboard and glue, or a base with slots for hold-downs to clamp the material. Fig 100. Heavy pieces of material, would normally be clamped using mechanical means. Small wooden objects can be adequately secured by using hot-melt glue on a base-board. Sheet material and laminates like plastics are best held down with a vacuum table.

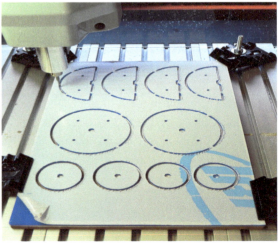

Fig 100: Slot and hold-down clamps

This CNC router is a very well equipped small free standing machine with a vacuum bed. Fig 101. The vacuum bed puts a significant cost on the overall purchase price. The vacuum pump is large and heavy - the vacuum pipes usually have to be plumbed in.

To enable the material to be machined to its full depth, a sacrificial baseboard is often used to allow the router to cut through the material without damaging the router table. I use either 12mm or 15mm MDF sheet as a sacrificial base. MDF has an even thickness and works with both mechanical and vacuum methods of material holding. The surface does not need preparing for a vacuum bed - the vacuum is strong enough to penetrate the MDF.

Cutting wood is quite straight-forward but securing it for cutting can be a problem. Solid wood is rarely perfectly flat (it tends to warp) and therefore both mechanical means and glue are recommended for fixing. I use a hot-melt glue gun to fix the material to my baseboard. It sets very quickly and has good strength. But most importantly it can be easily cleaned off afterwards enabling the baseboard to be re-used. See picture opposite Fig 102, using a vacuum table and hot-melt glue to secure the plank for machining.

Composite wooden sheet like plywood, block-board and MDF are all much easier to secure than solid wood. One can use much larger sheets that fit the whole baseboard of the CNC. They are very flat and easily secured with the vacuum table. Using the hold down method can lead to the material bowing in the middle, which will affect the machining.

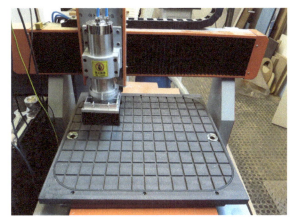

Fig 101: Vacuum Table

Fig 102: Material being glued to sacrificial based board

Extraction

When one uses the CNC for the first time its fascinating to watch the router cut the shapes automatically, unhindered by the chip extraction hood. For small operations like drilling, I rarely fit the extraction hood. But for all other operations I have the extractor hood fitted. Dust can damage your health.

The extractor hood has two purposes, the first and obvious one is to remove the chips from the cutter, the second is very important for cutting plastics - the forced air-flow cools the router blade.

The extractor hood that was supplied with my CNC was a huge metal enclosure. It was difficult to fit, hard to set the correct height of the router blade, and more importantly it was difficult to see what was happening. Fig 103.

Fig 103: Bulky extraction cowl

On the Internet I saw that an enthusiast had made his own extraction hood out of clear acrylic sheet. This seemed an excellent idea. I set about designing my own hood.

My first version had a clear acrylic top and a plastic skirt made from heavy-duty door screening plastic. I screwed the skirt onto the 10mm top cover using 4M bolts. I decided to extract through the back of the hood rather than the side - I had enough clearance under my router head. The hood worked reasonably well but the skirt was not very efficient.

So I redesigned the hood using door-draft brushes which came with an aluminium channel. This has proved to be a very practical and efficient design. Its more compact than the original metal one supplied, I can see what I am cutting, and the brush skirt allows me to access the router blade easily to set the datum height. The plans and build instructions for this hood are included in my Book 3 - '10 Simple projects to make.'

CNC Operation

With my Mach3 control system, I load the G-Code into the system and it quickly checks that it can all be read. There are so many variations of the G-Code used by CNC manufacturers that its a wise precaution to test the readability before starting.

The axes have been zeroed to the datum as explained earlier and the vacuum table and extraction switched on. The cycle can now start. Hopefully it will work through the G-Code without problem and the item machined as required.

However things often go wrong. A router cutter can break. The through holes may not cut deep enough. The toolpath has been wrongly specified etc. etc. So the CNC has to be stopped. Next comes the interesting problem. Do you want to retain the material and the datum and start again? It is very complicated to get the machine restarted half-way through its cycle. I have made so many mistakes restarting resulting in broken routers, damaged material or even worse holes in my baseboard!

I have a simple approach these days. Jog the router cutter head clear of the material and press the 'return to zero' button. This safely gets the cutter clear and retains the zero datum point. I can then correct the problem and start the cycle again from the start.

Only the very brave restart a cycle half-way through.

My CNC is so accurate that its not a problem reworking areas already machined, I can always increase the feed rate as no cutting is taking place. Then reset the feed rate once the uncut areas are approached.

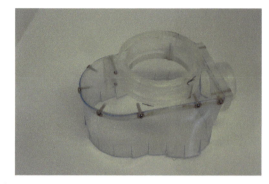

Fig 104: Home made router cover in clear plastic

Fig 105: Modified Router cover

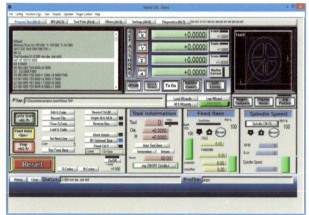

Fig 106: Mach3 Control Panel

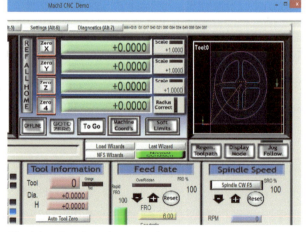

Fig 107: Setting the zero datum

Sometimes I have underestimated the feed rate in general cutting - say on long straight cuts. Mach3 allows me to increase the feed rate for these sections during the cycle and reset it back to the programmed rate if needed. Its the same with router spindle speed but this doesn't have to be changed very often.

Templates

During my college course I spent time with the CNC engineers at Ercol Furniture. One of the great things I learnt from them was the use of templates to cut both sides of the material.

I now use templates quite frequently. The secret of the template is a result of the CAM system being able to specify cutting an outside profile as well as an inside profile. As an example the Jewellry box project in Book 3 uses an oval lid. The lid has to be profiled and a lip cut on one side, and then a name is engraved on the other side and a bevel edge machined. Fig 108.

The machining of the underside, lip and profile are quite straightforward - see above. The CAM system is then reworked for the machining of the template and the other side of the lid. There are three operations all linked to the same datum. The cutting of the internal profile of the template; the engraving of the lid; and the cutting of the bevel around the edge.

Using a piece of scrap material the lid shape is then cut out as a separate operation using the inside profile plus an allowance of say 0.1mm - depending on the accuracy of your CNC. Fig 109. This ensures the lid can be slotted in and out of the template with a small clearance.

The previously machined lid is now placed in the template and secured with some hot-melt glue. Care being taken to keep the original zero datum used for the template. The template is then used to engrave the lid and cut the bevel along the edge. See opposite Fig 110. This example is explained in full in Book 3 Projects.

This can be a very accurate means of holding previously machined profiles for machining the reverse side.

Fig 108: Machining the jewellry box in Corian

Fig 109: Creating a holding template

Fig 110: Machining the reverse side

Setting up a new CNC Router

I have had to set up several new CNC Routers and have learnt a lot about their initial problems - which they all have.

All of my machines were made in China by different companies. Each one had significant setting-up problems. The big problem with buying these machines is support. Only one of the makes had a UK 'Consultant' to talk you through the problems of setting up. The others it was left to telephone calls on Skype and endless e-mails. 'Lost in translation' typifies the problem. Invariably the engineers do not speak English and an interpreter is appointed by the Chinese manufacturer who usually has no engineering ability to understand the problem you are describing. I tried to supplement my conversations with close-up pictures of the problem

Fig 111: So heavy I had to get a crane to unload it

I have eventually solved all the problems but it did take time - so be prepared for set-up issues.

The first problem I had with my machines was they had been damaged in transit. Both due to poor crating up of the machine and bad handling by the shippers. These machines are usually very heavy so they have to be secured well to the base of the wooden crate. Machines broke free from their bases and caused superficial damage.

The first machine was so heavy I had to hire a crane to lift it from the delivery truck. (Fig 111). The second machine had arrived in the UK safely but fell off the fork lift truck loading it into the delivery lorry. The machine had been placed at one side of the huge crate and lighter extraction equipment on the other side of the case. When the forks lifted it in the middle of the crate it fell over. Fig 113.

Fig 112: Damaged Router Cover

I did make considerable savings by buying direct from the manufacture in China, but at a cost later - I can see why machines sold in the UK by a distributor cost considerably more. My third CNC I did buy from a UK distributor and it was delivered without intact, it had connectivity problems which were quickly solved by the company's local technical support.

Talking afterwards to the importer they mentioned that they have no idea what the technical competence is of the person buying the machine. They are not able to provide training on how to use a CNC system

Fig 113. Damaged gantry cover

CNC Control System

As I mentioned earlier, some machines are supplied with the manufacturers own control system. Whilst this inevitably works, it is usually very limited in what it can do and can be expensive to buy add-ons like a remote controller.

My first CNC came with a free Chinese control system program and interface card. It was incredibly limited in what it could do and difficult to use. It was upgradeable to a more comprehensive version but at $1,000 it seemed very expensive. So I decided to use the famous Mach3 universal control system - low cost widely used, well proved, extensive help videos, lots of third-party add-ons and excellent online support. I fitted a new interface card, (I was an electronic engineer) and set up the software interface. I've never looked back.

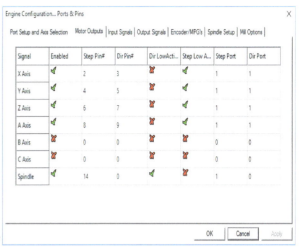

Fig 114: Setting up the CNC in Mach3

My other CNC machines were available with the Mach3 operating system, which I already understood.

Setting up the CNC control system for the first time can be a bit daunting. Luckily Mach3 has a series of excellent video tutorials that show you how to do it. The same Mach3 interface card was used in my last two CNC's and it also had an excellent manual, in English and Chinese, on how to set up the control system. Unfortunately the manual could not anticipate the specification of the stepping motors or the various limiters so these had to be configured by trial and error. Fig 114.

During the configuration the measurement basis is set (millimetres or inches), the home limits are set, the motors are set and the cutter acceleration is set. Fig 115.

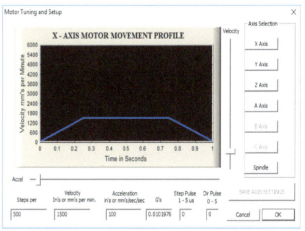

Fig 115: Configuring the stepping motors

Be careful when switching the CNC on for the first time - it can be very quick to bury the cutting head into the baseboard before you have time to hit the panic button. I now prefer to use a test G-Code sample rather than my own to eliminate unnecessary variables.

The alignment of the CNC bed

During shipping things get slightly out of alignment. So in all cases I check to bed for flatness and the axes for accuracy. Both of my first CNCs had their heads damaged and knocked slightly out of alignment. I checked that the router motor was vertically aligned and adjusted it if necessary.

The vacuum tables supplied all have a thick black composite table material, made form old car types, as the bed. It is very easy to machine. (Fig 116). Usually the vacuum bed is cut out

Fig 116: Router used for bed alignment

insitu by the CNC before shipping to ensure it is flat and in line. Things can move in shipping. My first machine developed a depression in the centre of the base board - this could be roughly adjusted underneath the bed by adjusting the supporting bolts. I was able to get it quite close to true then took a wide surface finishing router cutter, opposite, and trued the whole bed by only taking about 1.5mm off the high points.

Its essential that the bed is true especially when you are cutting thin laminates.

Checking the stepping motor accuracy

The next major problem is ensuring your CNC is cutting accurately - you down want oval shaped round holes! Mach3 has an excellent facility for testing the accuracy of the X Y and Z axes. I usually set a 600mm steel rule on the base and zero the router cutter (with an engraving point fitted) at one end and set the CNC to move 600mm. You then insert the distance actually traversed and try again until its accurate to 1mm in 600mm in my case. I reset the z axis using a vernier depth gauge the same method. Fig 118 and 119.

This program resets the stepping motors to ensure they are responding accurately to the G-Code instructions given.

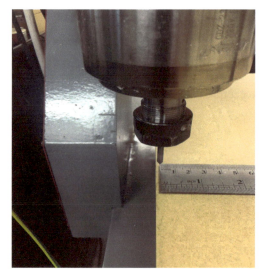

Fig 117: Using a steel rule to check stepping motor accuracy

Fig 118: Mach3 setting steps per axis

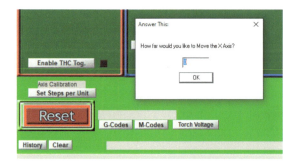

Fig 119: Mach3 stepping distance entry